Published by: Boulder Press, P.O. Box 1583, Solana Beach, CA 92075

Photography and Text © 2013 Mike Barton. Photographer's website: www.mikebartonphoto.com

Individual prints may be purchased directly from the photographer: cell phone (720) 934-4322

Editor: David L. Miles, Co-director Harsha House Museum, Charlevoix (Michigan) Historical Society

Library of Congress Control Number: 2013916079

ISBN 13: 978-0-9899268-0-5
ISBN 10: 0-9899268-0-X
First Printing: 2013
Printed in China

San Diego's North Coast

DEL MAR · SOLANA BEACH · CARDIFF-BY-THE-SEA · ENCINITAS

photography and text by Mike Barton

BOULDER PRESS

CONTENTS

ABOVE: The view from the San Elijo State Beach Campground in Cardiff-by-the-Sea looking south to Solana Beach and Del Mar.
OPPOSITE PAGE: If you want to see a dog with a big smile, look no further. Nani the Bernese Mountain Dog is one of many dogs who showcase their special surfing talents at the annual Surf-a-Thon on Dog Beach in Del Mar. In addition to her surfing skills, Nani was on the cover of the 2010 Surf Dog Calendar.

INTRODUCTION

Sprinkled along the coastline roughly twenty miles north of San Diego are four unique seaside villages with a small-town feel: Del Mar, Solana Beach, Cardiff-by-the-Sea and Encinitas. North County is a place where you can actually find a place to park near the beach without having to circle the block fifty times.

With many affluent neighborhoods, North County is the most expensive area of San Diego. A postcard found in a local store shows a one-room shack with the caption, "One million dollar fixer upper." That might be a stretch but you will quickly get the idea when you look at the price of real estate in the area.

Like most beach towns, everything seems to revolve around the ocean. Beach culture is very important in the area - everyone seems to be a little more laid back.

Outdoor enthusiasts have no problem staying entertained, from hiking at Torrey Pines to biking along Coast Highway 101 to running on the beach to surfing. With miles of pristine coastline, majestic bluffs and secluded coves, it is an ideal spot to live or visit.

The downtowns are at bluff level but are all within easy walking distance to the beach. The further up the coast you go, the more beachy the towns get.

LEFT: Woodie cars from decades past are common along the coast where the motto is "Old Guys Rule."

BELOW: The summer racing season at Del Mar Race Track adds excitement to the entire community.

OPPOSITE PAGE: You can go up in a paraglider or hang glider from the Torrey Pines Gliderport and soar over the coast. Torrey Pines Golf Course is the patch of green above the bluff.

RIGHT: The San Elijo Lagoon river mouth in Cardiff-by-the-Sea.

OPPOSITE PAGE AND BELOW: Low tide and saturated sand make it possible to photograph sunset reflections on the beach.

ABOVE: Sand dredged from an offshore vessel is pumped onto the beaches to keep them from eroding during winter storms.

LEFT: Surf fishing is popular all along the coast. Some of the common fish catches include Barred Surf Perch, Croaker, Corbina, Halibut and Bat Ray.

OPPOSITE PAGE TOP: A 315-foot-long vessel named the *Liberty Island* hopper dredge, shown off the shore of Dog Beach, is used to replenish sand on many beaches in North County.

RIGHT: Children play as surfers head toward the ocean on Seaside Beach in Cardiff-by-the-Sea.

BELOW: Surfing looms large along the coast.

OPPOSITE PAGE: The craggy bluffs along the tracks in south Del Mar turn a brilliant orange as the sun begins to set. The village of La Jolla is the point in the distance on the far right.

ABOVE: During low tide at Swami's Beach in Encinitas, the extensive "Swami's Reef" and tide pools become visible.

RIGHT: One of several caves carved into the bluffs by the surf near Tide Beach Park in Solana Beach.

OPPOSITE PAGE: This labyrinth on the

LEFT AND BELOW: Beach volleyball is popular in Southern California and is a common sight at Moonlight Beach (left) in Encinitas and Dog Beach (below) in Del Mar.

OPPOSITE PAGE TOP: Paddleboarders come and go as the sun sets on Cardiff State Beach.

OPPOSITE PAGE BOTTOM: High bluffs dominate the shores of Solana Beach in this view looking north from Fletcher Cove Beach.

LEFT: Scripps Bluff Preserve, perched above Dog Beach on the north end of Del Mar, is a popular destination for the Frogs Fitness and RossFit famed "Beach Workout."

BELOW: The surf report at the Del Mar Lifeguard Station.

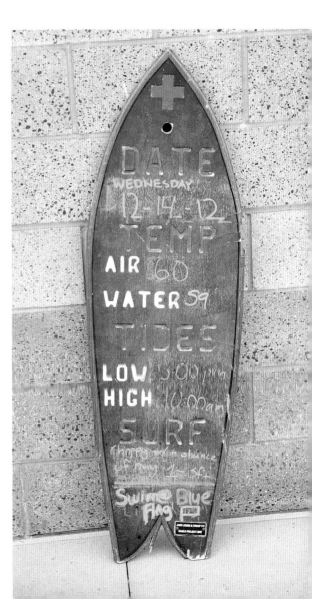

ABOVE: Built in 1927, Stratford Square is Del Mar's most historic and recognizable building.
OPPOSITE PAGE: Powerhouse Park is a popular seaside park nestled below the downtown.

DEL MAR

Del Mar is an affluent beach town with natural elegance just twenty miles north of San Diego.

When the California Southern Railroad tracks were laid down between San Diego and Los Angeles in 1882, they went smack through where Del Mar is today. The contractor on the project, Theodore M. Loop, liked the area so much that he built a home and established a tent city on the beach. Loop's wife named it Del Mar from the popular poem of the time titled "The Fight of Paseo Del Mar."

Around the same time, Loop approached Colonel Jacob Taylor with the idea of building a town in the area. Taylor, a wealthy rancher, saw great potential and envisioned Del Mar as a seaside resort for the rich and famous.

In 1885, Taylor purchased 338 acres for $1,000 and began developing a resort town. You can't rent a studio apartment in town for that much nowadays.

Along with forty homes and two schools, Taylor built a resort hotel, train depot, dance hall and a large bathing pool on the ocean. As a result, Del Mar quickly became an elegant vacation destination that attracted silent movie stars from Hollywood.

LEFT: The view from Scripps Bluff Preserve above Dog Beach stretches from the beaches along Del Mar to La Jolla in the distance.

PAGE 26: Since 1983, summer twilight concerts have been a Del Mar tradition. Come down to Powerhouse Park with your blankets and lawn chairs to picnic and enjoy live music as the sun sets over the ocean.

PAGE 27: Jake's Del Mar and the Poseidon Restaurant have oceanfront views.

ABOVE: The view from the popular Brigantine Restaurant overlooks the Del Mar Race Track. On the right side of the photo, horses can be seen rounding the last turn on the Jimmy Durante Turf Course.

Del Mar is "Where The Turf Meets The Surf." Bing Crosby recorded "Where The Turf Meets The Surf" in 1937 to promote the new Del Mar Race Track. It's been the slogan for the track as well as the town ever since.

RIGHT: An artist captures the cliffs of Crest Canyon in Del Mar. The white buildings in the distance are the condominiums in Solana Beach that overlook the Del Mar Fairgrounds.

OPPOSITE PAGE: Powerhouse Park (bottom) and the Powerhouse Community Center (top) are the result of a 17-year project that started in 1983. The original powerhouse, built in 1928, had huge boilers that supplied hot water and heat for the Stratford Inn and its pool.

ABOVE, OPPOSITE PAGE AND PAGE 35: The Del Mar Plaza has a great collection of restaurants and shops with European flavor and wonderful ocean views. The multilevel plaza has tiled fountains, cobblestone pathways and magnificent archways.

LEFT: The Del Mar Train Station (1910) still exists, but trains don't stop there anymore.

BELOW: Free Flight, established 1981, is an exotic bird sanctuary in Del Mar. Bird lovers can see and hear the colorful birds in this open-air tropical oasis.

OPPOSITE PAGE TOP: The Del Mar Fairgrounds host The San Diego County Fair from early June to the Fourth of July.

OPPOSITE PAGE BOTTOM LEFT: Opening day at the track is highlighted by the unique Fabulous Hats Contest.

The Helen Woodward Animal Center's annual Puppy Love 5K is a fundraiser to help orphaned animals. Kevin Bacon (above left), the Juliana pig, draws attention from a fellow competitor.

OPPOSITE PAGE: The annual Red Nose Run (5K) takes place on Del Mar Beach near Powerhouse Park on a Friday afternoon in mid-December.

ABOVE: The view from Del Mar Plaza. Stratford Square on the left was a popular hangout for Hollywood stars during the 1930s and 1940s.

LEFT: Looks like a tropical island but it's Del Mar.

OPPOSITE PAGE BOTTOM: The view from Del Mar looking north towards the high bluffs overlooking Dog Beach and up the coast to Encinitas.

ABOVE: A flock of the once endangered California brown pelican soars towards Scripps Bluff Preserve.
OPPOSITE PAGE: Del Mar Beach is popular for sunbathing, surfing, walking and all kinds of beach games.

ABOVE: Fireworks on July 4 signal the end of the season for the annual San Diego County Fair.
OPPOSITE PAGE: Stratford Square (top) and the Holiday of Lights at the Del Mar Fairgrounds (bottom).

ABOVE: The San Dieguito River Mouth meets the sea at Dog Beach and is a place where dogs can swim without the waves.
OPPOSITE PAGE: Another view of Del Mar Beach (top) and Dog Beach (bottom).

SOLANA BEACH

Solana Beach is a bustling little city tucked between Del Mar and Cardiff-by-the-Sea with a perfect small-town atmosphere and coastal charm. Although it is one of California's smallest cities, it has a lot to offer.

The area began to develop in the early 1920s when Colonel Ed Fletcher purchased 140 acres from farmer George H. Jones for $20 an acre. At the time, the high bluffs prevented access to the beach so Fletcher decided to cut a notch in the cliff. Using a fire hose and high pressure water, it took one man three months to complete the task. As a result, the park and adjacent beach were named Fletcher Cove in the colonel's honor.

Although most of the 1.7 miles of coastline is dominated by cliffs near the water's edge, you won't have much trouble finding your way to the beach. In 2003, Solana Beach became the first city in the nation to ban smoking on its beaches.

All along Coast Highway 101 and the trendy Cedros Design District is where you will find shops, restaurants and galleries. The centrally located Solana Beach Train Station gets you where you need to go.

PAGE 48: The Solana Beach Train Station, designed by architect Wellington Quigley, was built in 1995 to replace the Del Mar train depot. Quigley's design was inspired by a group of 1940 Quonset huts on South Cedros Avenue a few blocks from the station. They still exist along the Cedros Design District.

LEFT: The Leaping Lotus in the heart of the Design District is one of the area's most unique shopping environments with over 120 merchants.

PAGE 49: The south entrance to the Coastal Rail Trail runs along Coast Highway 101 and the train tracks. The 1.5 mile trail, first completed in 2005, is popular with runners, roller bladers, cyclists, and dog walkers.

OPPOSITE PAGE BOTTOM: The beach, where these folks are heading, is just a few blocks from the Design District.

Images from Tide Beach Park on the north end of Solana Beach.

LEFT: This colorful winding path leads you to Mabel's Clothing & Gifts.

OPPOSITE PAGE COUNTERCLOCKWISE: Lynne Merchant Jewelry, Bellinis Antique Italia, Cow Parade by artist Rina Vinetz and bike art in front of Claire's on Cedros.

ABOVE LEFT: You will find the latest and greatest products for your pup at Muttropolis.

ABOVE RIGHT: During the racing season, a double-decker bus shuttles people between the train station and Del Mar Race Track.

OPPOSITE PAGE AND RIGHT: Cedros Gardens has been at its current location on S. Cedros Avenue since 1994.

Images of Fletcher Cove Park, a
grassy park with a playground,
picnic tables and a ramp down to
the beach.
Fletcher Cove has summer
concerts, festivals and is a popular
gathering place for families.
The nickname for the beach,
"Pillbox," originated from the
military pillbox or bunker
appearance of the concrete seawall
that once protected the bluffs.

ABOVE: The view from the condominiums along Sierra Avenue.
OPPOSITE PAGE: The Green Flash Brewery truck (top) and the Sunday farmers market (top right and bottom).

ABOVE: Many establishments got a facelift during the Highway 101 Westside Improvement Project in 2012-13.

RIGHT: One of several colorful buildings on S. Cedros Avenue.

OPPOSITE PAGE TOP: Solana Beach's own Atomic Groove makes an appearance at the annual Fiesta Del Sol.

OPPOSITE PAGE BELOW: It's the end of the weekend for these beachgoers as they head up the ramp from Fletcher Cove Beach.

BELOW: Solo is a popular interior design store on S. Cedros Aveune.

ABOVE AND OPPOSITE PAGE TOP: Tide Beach Park is a secluded beach by the bluffs at the north end of Solana Beach.

LEFT: The stairway to Tide Beach Park. The outer reef called Table Tops is well known for surfing, snorkeling and fishing.

OPPOSITE PAGE BOTTOM: This sign above the Solana Beach Chamber of Commerce has been lighting up Solana Beach since 1950.

ABOVE: The view looking south from the San Elijo State Beach Campground.
OPPOSITE PAGE: Runners and cyclists share Coast Highway 101 as they enter Cardiff-by-the-Sea from Solana Beach.
PAGE 70-71: San Elijo State Beach sits along the bluffs below the campground.

CARDIFF-BY-THE-SEA

Cardiff-by-the-Sea is a classic beach community located north of Solana Beach. The city features a unique oceanfront campground, pristine beaches for its hardcore surfing community and a surfer statue that gets dressed up while no one is looking.

The Mackinnon family settled on the north shore of the San Elijo Lagoon in 1875 and became successful farmers. When a Boston painter named J. Frank Cullen arrived in the area in 1910, he envisioned the land cultivated by the Mackinnons as a seaside playground.

Cullen bought a large chunk of land and began to develop a town. In 1912, he built a hotel overlooking the bluff, an ocean pier and a bathhouse. He named his new town "Cardiff-by-the-Sea" after Cardiff, Wales where his wife was from.

If you look closely, you will notice that many streets have English names such as Birmingham, Oxford, Chesterfield and Manchester.

Cardiff by the Sea has become the seaside playground Cullen had hoped but still maintains its small town hospitality.

OPPOSITE PAGE TOP:
The Coaster train
runs along the coast
between Oceanside and
downtown San Diego.
Bikers, runners and
walkers enjoy the seaside
scenery on the path along
Coast Highway 101.

ABOVE. The Cardiff-by-the-Sea Library had its grand opening in 2003. The original library opened in a grocery store a few blocks away in 1914.

OPPOSITE PAGE: Seaside Beach (top) is located on the south end of town next to Coast Highway 101 and George's Beach (bottom) stretches in front of Restaurant Row.

ABOVE. Cardiff Reef Beach at Tower 16 is a popular surfing spot where the bluff ends south of the campground near the San Elijo Lagoon river mouth.

LEFT AND ABOVE: The iconic and controversial "Cardiff Kook" statue has rested along Coast Highway 101 for all to see since 2007. Sculptor Matthew Antichevich named his $92,000 creation the "Magic Carpet Ride" but local surfers had other ideas and gave it a nickname that has seemed to stick.

The statue is often dressed up in everything from a simple bikini top to Santa Claus during Christmas. But two of the most creative pranks have been a prehistoric setting with a pterodactyl swooping down on the statue, and a huge "Jaws"-like papier mâché shark ready to swallow up the surfer from below.

RIGHT: Pipes Cafe was named after a popular surfing spot called "Pipes" on the north end of the campground.

BELOW: The turquoise building in the background was once home to Kook's Cafe.

The San Elijo Lagoon is one of the county's few remaining coastal wetlands. The lagoon's mouth flows to the ocean. As you walk the shallow-water estuary's eight miles of trails, you may encounter as many as 300 species of birds, 16 species of reptiles and amphibians, 26 species of mammals and 300 species of plants. There is a nature center on the north side of the lagoon that details the lagoon's plant and animal communities, ecology and Native American history. The county has done a good job protecting the wetlands and they have remained relatively undeveloped as a result.

ABOVE: The view of the San Elijo Lagoon looking south over the train tracks that run through the lagoon.

OPPOSITE PAGE: Many homes in Cardiff overlook the coastal wetlands.

LEFT AND BELOW:
This winding tree-lined path was once a weed-infested vacant lot along the railroad tracks near Seaside Market. The area, now called Carpentier Parkway, has been transformed into a walkway filled with flowers and drought-resistant plants, thanks to the Cardiff Botanical Society.

OPPOSITE PAGE:
The view looking north from the San Elijo State Beach Campground.

RIGHT: The temporary San Elijo lifeguard tower will be replaced with a permanent tower in 2015. The original tower, built in the 1960s, was dismantled after erosion left it dangerously close to the edge of the bluff.

BELOW: The view looking south towards Swami's Beach in Encinitas.

OPPOSITE PAGE: This photo was taken five minutes before the one on page 85 and from the exact same spot.

ABOVE: Wildflowers fill the open space along Coast Highway 101 south of the San Elijo Lagoon.

RIGHT: Las Olas is a popular Mexican restaurant across from the beach.

OPPOSITE PAGE: The view looking south from the deck of the Pacific Coast Grill, one of three oceanfront restaurants in Cardiff. The umbrella-filled patio belongs to the Beach House Restaurant.

ENCINITAS

Encinitas is a laid back beach town with six miles of rugged coastline.

Surfing is huge here. National Geographic named Encinitas one of the World's 20 Best Surf Towns, no other SoCal town made the list. It's also the home of Hansen's Surf Shop, San Diego's oldest surfboard store that began in a little shack on North Shore, Oahu in 1961.

The name Encinitas comes from Encina Canada, Spanish for "hills of live oaks" after a 1669 expedition noted all the live oaks that dotted the hills in the area.

In 1881, Jabez Pitcher settled in Encinitas and claimed 160 acres by the railroad tracks near D Street. Pitcher is considered to be the city's founding father.

Historic Coast Highway 101 runs right through a downtown that remains relatively unchanged and unspoiled while keeping up with current times.

Swami's Beach is an area on the south end of Encinitas named after the Self-Realization Fellowship founded by Swami Paramahansa Yogananda in 1937. Swami's Beach is a surfer's haven (left) and the golden domes of the Self-Realization Fellowship (below) are Encinitas's most recognizable structures.

LEFT: The view looking south from Moonlight Beach. The ship in the distance is the *Liberty Island* hopper dredge that is used to replenish sand on the beach.

BELOW: In 2011, Encinitas woodcarver Tim Richards transformed a ten-foot-tall Torrey pine stump at Swami's Park into a tiki head. The 80-year-old Torrey pine fell victim to a bark beetle infestation and was cut down a few months before Richards went to work on it.

OPPOSITE PAGE TOP: Pannikin Coffee and Tea is located in this historic Santa Fe Railroad Station built in 1888. The building served as the original train station for Encinitas until it closed in 1969. Before it was moved to its current location in the early 1970s, the building was located near the Lumberyard shopping center.

RIGHT: The Surfing Madonna found a permanent home in 2012 on a wall between Café Ipe and Surfy Surfy. The 10 by 10-foot mosaic, created by artist Mark Patterson, depicts the Virgin of Guadalupe surfing. The controversial artwork first appeared in April, 2011 under the train bridge near Encinitas Blvd. But since the installer didn't go through the normal review process, the mosaic was labeled as graffiti and the city ordered it to be removed. The Surfing Madonna sat in storage until finding its new home.

BELOW RIGHT: As you enter downtown Encinitas on Coast Highway 101 from the north, you are greeted by this bronze sculpture of a young girl waving her hand. The statue, known as the "Encinitas Child," was created by nationally renowned artist and local resident Manuelita Brown.

ABOVE: The Encinitas Library opened in 2008.

RIGHT: Wavecrest, the world's largest gathering of vintage wood-paneled vehicles, is held every September on Moonlight Beach.

OPPOSITE PAGE TOP: The northern section of downtown has retained some of its historical look in contrast to the redeveloped southern end of town.

OPPOSITE PAGE BOTTOM: Downtown Encinitas is lined by old woodies, hotrods and other vintage cars on Classic Car Nights held every third Thursday during the summer

LEFT: Swami's is one of several California surfing spots mentioned in the Beach Boys hit "Surfin' USA."

BELOW: The popular Encinitas Holiday Parade held in December.

OPPOSITE PAGE TOP: The view of Swami's from the San Elijo State Beach Campground.

OPPOSITE PAGE BOTTOM: The sun sets over the sea and K Street in Encinitas.

Moonlight State Beach is a popular place for sunbathing and volleyball. The beach is also host to the Sunday Concerts by the Sea. It got its name from the midnight picnics that locals had on the beach in the early 1900s.

OPPOSITE PAGE TOP LEFT: One of 16 mosaic sewer covers found along the downtown sidewalks in Encinitas. Artist Terry Weaver designed each one to portray a different Encinitas scene.

OPPOSITE PAGE TOP: The Self-Realization Fellowship Meditation Gardens sit on a bluff with views of the ocean. The tranquil gardens feature waterfalls and koi ponds.

OPPOSITE PAGE BOTTOM: A black lab negotiates the waves and slippery reef at Swami's Beach.

RIGHT: It's hard to miss the Golden Lotus Tower of the Self-Realization Fellowship Center on the south end of Encinitas.

BELOW LEFT: The Self-Realization Fellowship Temple was built in 1916 at Third and E Street and served as an elementary school until 1936. The temple was moved to its current location on Second Street in 1953.

BELOW RIGHT: The Old School House. This one-room schoolhouse (1883) is home to the Encinitas Historical Society.

Beacon's Beach is a small
cove on the north end of
Encinitas in a community
called Leucadia. The
beach, known for its
surfing, is accessible by
a series of switchbacks
down the bluff.
Because of its secluded
location, it feels like
a secret spot and it's
definitely a local's beach.
The official name is
Leucadia State Beach but
locals have been calling it
Beacon's for so long they
don't remember why. Even
the sign at the entrance
reads Beacon's.

OPPOSITE PAGE TOP AND PAGE 91: The La Paloma Theater opened in 1928 and was one of the first theaters to show "talkies" after Warner Bros. introduced talking pictures in 1927.

LEFT: The Boat Houses are just two blocks from the beach but they have never been to sea. They were built in the late 1920s by Miles Kellogg from materials recycled from the 1888 Moonlight Beach Dance Parlor.

BELOW: On the south end of town you will find Swami's Cafe and Flower Frenzy.

SURFING

World-class surfing for all levels can be found along the California coastline and San Diego's north coast is no exception. The Beach Boys made reference to La Jolla, Del Mar and Swami's in their iconic hit "Surfin' USA."

Surfing has influenced the entire beach culture and people who don't even surf understand how the sport identifies this area.

Rain or shine, summer or winter, you will find surfers riding the waves all along the coast. For many, surfing is more than just a sport; it's a way of life. For some it's just a long lunch break.

There seems to be a surf shop around every corner. You will find that many of the restaurants and other establishments are surf-themed and surf fashion is more common than not.

PAGE 115: The surfboard
storage shed behind
Mitch's Surf Shop (1967)
in Solana Beach.

RIGHT: The sport of stand
up paddle (SUP) boarding
became the fastest growing
water sport in the nation
after being introduced in
California by legendary
Hawaiian surfer Rick
Thomas in 2000.

BELOW: Tower 19 in
Cardiff-by-the-Sea.

OPPOSITE PAGE: Ten
surfers share the same
wave at Swami's.

ABOVE LEFT: Surfer crossings like this one near Beacon's Beach are common in the area.

LEFT AND OPPOSITE PAGE: Young surfers participate in the National Scholastic Surfing Association contest at Seaside Beach in Cardiff-by-the-Sea.

PAGE 118: One of the six stairways to the beach from the San Elijo State Campground.

OPPOSITE PAGE: Sur-fur Ricochet, or Ricki for short, took first place at the 2013 Surf Dog Surf-A-Thon on Dog Beach. Ricki has helped raise almost $300,000 at several fundraising events. Check out her website: www.surfdogricochet.com.

DOG BEACH

North Beach, affectionately called "Dog Beach" by locals, is located on the north end of Del Mar directly west of the Del Mar Race Track. You will find every kind of dog imaginable, from the little dachshund to the fearless Dalmatian.

When dogs are allowed off-leash after Labor Day to mid June, tennis balls fly and Frisbees fling. Big dogs chase little dogs and little dogs chase big dogs. If you want to see a dog smile, this is the place.

As cars with dogs arrive at the beach, you can't help but notice the reaction of the dogs - their tails begin to wag wildly and their eyes become focused on the beach in the distance. They can hardly contain themselves as they wait for their owners to park and let them free.

Before floods washed away the horse trail from the race track to this beach in the early 1980s, trainers and owners would take horses to the ocean because the cold salt water was believed to be very therapeutic.

ABOVE: At low tide, the playground for the dogs expands and they get a chance to play on the exposed reef.

RIGHT: These steps lead to Scripps Bluff Preserve and some of the best views in the area.

ABOVE: Dog Beach is so wide that dogs don't mind sharing it with humans.

RIGHT: Even if you don't have a dog, it's fun to just watch dogs chasing each other and fetching tennis balls in the surf.

TRACK SEASON

Bing Crosby loved horse racing and was instrumental in the development of the Del Mar Race Track. Actors Pat O'Brien and Oliver Hardy (of Laurel & Hardy) were among the original partners.

When the track opened in 1937, Crosby greeted the first fans through the gate. With Crosby leading the way, Del Mar quickly became a summer destination for many Hollywood stars.

Some of the summer regulars back then included Lucille Ball, Desi Arnaz, Betty Grable, Mickey Rooney, Jimmy Durante, W. C. Fields, Ava Gardner, Red Skelton and FBI director J. Edgar Hoover. Durante was around so much that the grass turf course and boulevard around the track were named in his honor.

Seabiscuit put the Del Mar Race Track on the map when he won the famous $25,000 winner-take-all race in 1938. Charles S. Howard, the owner of Seabiscuit, was one of the original partners of the track.

PAGE 131: Ladies don their best hats on opening day.

OPPOSITE PAGE AND PAGE 130: Before each race, it's customary for jockeys, owners and their guests to gather in the paddock area.

LEFT AND BELOW: Home stretch with the Solana Beach hillsides in the background.

ABOVE: Over 2000 multicolored jerseys hang in the Silk Room.

LEFT AND OPPOSITE PAGE BELOW: Horses are assembled, saddled, and paraded in the paddock area before each race.

ABOVE: The view from a paraglider over the Torrey Pines Gliderport looking south towards the curving coastline of La Jolla.

ABOVE: Eddie V's in La Jolla may have the best view of any establishment in San Diego County. Kayaking into the La Jolla sea caves is an unforgettable adventure.

SURROUNDING AREAS

Torrey Pines Golf Course (1957) is situated on the towering coastal cliffs overlooking the ocean in the community of La Jolla. Paragliders and hang gliders from the Torrey Pines Gliderport hover over the course throughout the day. The 36-hole municipal course was built on the site of Camp Callan, a U.S. Army training center during World War II. Owned by the city of San Diego, the course is host to the PGA Tour's annual Farmers Insurance Open (above) and was the site of the 2008 U.S Open won by Tiger Woods.

RANCHO SANTE FE

Just a few miles from the coast through winding roads lined with eucalyptus trees is the community of Rancho Santa Fe. Known as "The Ranch" by locals, the village is mainly residential with a charming downtown.

During the period from 1923-1929, homes were built on large parcels of land in the rolling hills among citrus and avocado groves. The Rancho Santa Fe Association (1927) adopted a Protective Covenant to maintain the aesthetics of this pleasant 6,200-acre community within Rancho Santa Fe.

This historic part of Rancho Santa Fe became known as "The Covenant" and is now home to sprawling country estates and is considered to be the wealthiest community in the nation.

ABOVE: A citrus orchard on Del Dios Ranch.
BELOW: The village center, built during the 1920s and 1930s, was influenced by Spanish and Mediterranean architecture.

LA JOLLA

Often considered to be the jewel of Southern California due to its dramatic coastline and quaint Mediterranean village atmosphere, La Jolla is an affluent seaside community south of Del Mar.

It's no surprise that La Jolla is one of California's most popular destinations. It's a place where you can indulge yourself with world-class shopping, luxurious hotels and one-of-a-kind dining. But it's the beaches that may be the biggest reason people flock to the village, especially in the summer.

La Jolla first became known as a resort area in the 1890s when the railroad connected it to San Diego. The area featured a bathhouse and dance hall to attract visitors along with cottages to encourage longer stays.

ABOVE: This road from the village area leads down to the grassy Scripps Park, the La Jolla Cove and other beaches.

RIGHT: The beach below Scripps Park is just a short walk down from the heart of the village.

CARLSBAD

Located just north of Encinitas is the seaside town of Carlsbad. Sometimes referred to as "The Village by the Sea" by locals, Carlsbad has an appealing downtown filled with cafes, antique shops and boutiques.

In the 1880s, Carlsbad was a whistle stop on the California Southern Railroad. At that time, a former ship's captain named John Frazier dug a well and tapped into a mineral springs. The well became a popular spot for train passengers and a major marketing campaign to attract visitors led to a period of rapid growth.

The town got its name after tests done on the water indicated that it was chemically similar to that in a famous health spa in Karlsbad, Bohemia.

ABOVE: This historic Victorian was built by Alonzo Culver in 1887 for Gerhard Schutte, president of the Carlsbad Land and Mineral Water Company. One of his partners, D.D. Wadsworth, built a mirror image of the home 200 feet away. In 1919 the new owner of the two Victorian homes renamed them the Twin Inns. The Wadsworth house was torn down in 1950 to make room for parking and the other twin, originally owned by Schutte, is now the Ocean House restaurant.

RIGHT: The Old Santa Fe Train Depot was built in 1887 and serviced Carlsbad until 1960. The gabled Victorian still sits next to its original location beside the tracks and now houses the Carlsbad Visitors Center.

TORREY PINES STATE NATURAL RESERVE

Just south of Del Mar is Torrey Pines State Natural Reserve, a 2000-acre coastal state park that has remained relatively unspoiled.

This area is the home of the Torrey pine, the rarest pine species in the United States. It now only grows here and on Santa Rosa Island off the coast of Santa Barbara.

The reserve features eight miles easy to moderate hiking trails through the wind-sculpted pines and deep ravines to the headlands overlooking the ocean.

BELOW: The end of the half-mile trail to Broken Hill Overlook comes to a precariously narrow point near the edge of the cliff.

Other Photo Books By Mike Barton

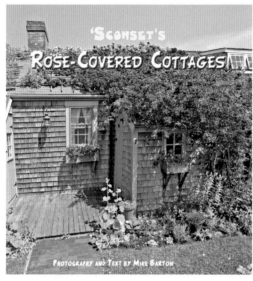

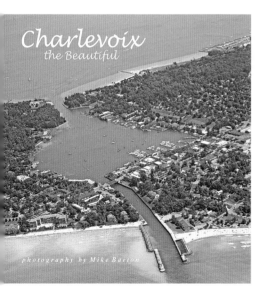

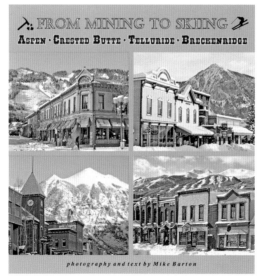

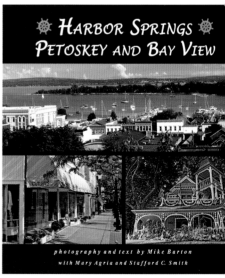

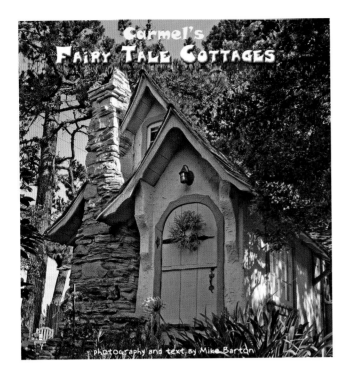

Carmel's FAIRY TALE COTTAGES

photography and text by Mike Barton

The MUSHROOM HOUSES of Charlevoix

photography and text by Mike Barton
with David L. Miles and Jeannine Wallace

A BOUT THE P HOTOGRAPHER

Mike Barton is a landscape photographer from Solana Beach, California. A native of Michigan, Mike moved to sunny California after graduating from Michigan State and began to photograph the Pacific coast. Michigan is a great place to "be from."

Photography became a true passion when he moved to Boulder, Colorado where he tried to photograph every square inch of the Colorado mountains.

Mike moved to San Diego from Boulder in 2010. He began this project, his ninth book, when he settled in Solana Beach in 2012.

Many people comment on the vibrant colors that Mike is able to bring out in his photographs. This requires returning to the same place over and over until the light and other conditions are just right A photo can be taken of the same location on different days and the clouds, colors, waves and reflections can vary dramatically.

To see more of Mike's work, please visit his website: www.mikebartonphoto.com.